U.S.A. TRAVEL GUIDES

NEW MEXICO

BY ANN HEINRICHS • ILLUSTRATED BY MATT KANIA

The Child's World®
childsworld.com

Published by The Child's World®
1980 Lookout Drive • Mankato, MN 56003-1705
800-599-READ • www.childsworld.com

Photo Credits

Copyright

ISBN 9781503819719
LCCN 2016961185

Printing

Printed in the United States of America
PA02334

Ann Heinrichs is the author of more than 100 books for children and young adults. She has also enjoyed successful careers as a children's book editor and an advertising copywriter. Ann grew up in Fort Smith, Arkansas, and lives in Chicago, Illinois.

post card

About the Author
Ann Heinrichs

Matt Kania loves maps and, as a kid, dreamed of making them. In school he studied geography and cartography, and today he makes maps for a living. Matt's favorite thing about drawing maps is learning about the places they represent. Many of the maps he has created can be found in books, magazines, videos, Web sites, and public places.

post card

About the
Map Illustrator
Matt Kania

On the Cover: The Taos Pueblo is home to approximately 150 people.

OUR NEW MEXICO TRIP

NEW MEXICO

How about a trip through New Mexico? You're sure to have a great time!

You'll meet Geronimo and Billy the Kid. You'll explore forests, deserts, and caves. You'll see kangaroo rats and wild pigs. You'll even learn about visitors from outer space!

Are you curious? Then hop aboard and buckle your seat belt. We're off on a big adventure!

WELCOME TO
NEW MEXICO

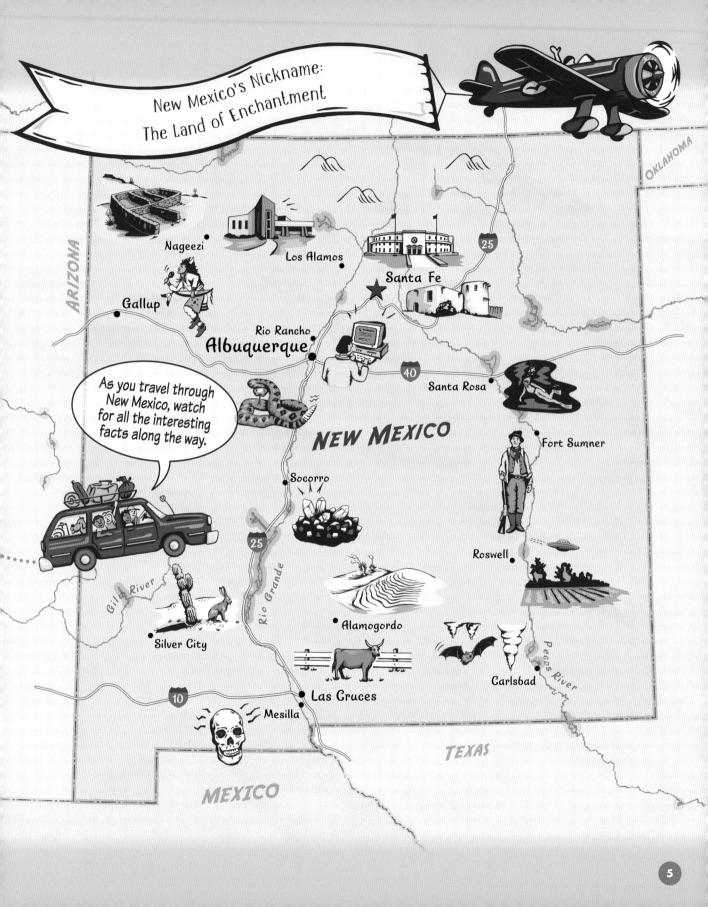

New Mexico's Nickname:
The Land of Enchantment

As you travel through New Mexico, watch for all the interesting facts along the way.

ARIZONA

OKLAHOMA

Nageezi

Los Alamos

Santa Fe

Gallup

Rio Rancho

Albuquerque

Santa Rosa

NEW MEXICO

Fort Sumner

Socorro

Roswell

Gila River

Rio Grande

Silver City

Alamogordo

Carlsbad

Pecos River

Las Cruces

Mesilla

TEXAS

MEXICO

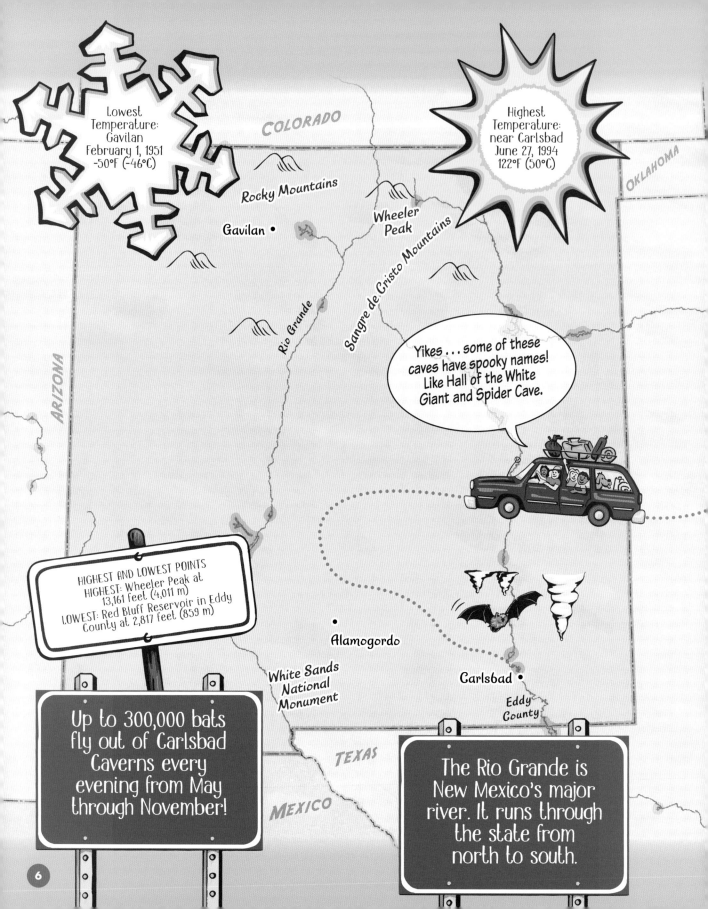

Lowest Temperature: Gavilan
February 1, 1951
-50°F (-46°C)

Highest Temperature: near Carlsbad
June 27, 1994
122°F (50°C)

COLORADO

OKLAHOMA

Rocky Mountains

Wheeler Peak

Gavilan •

Sangre de Cristo Mountains

Rio Grande

ARIZONA

Yikes . . . some of these caves have spooky names! Like Hall of the White Giant and Spider Cave.

HIGHEST AND LOWEST POINTS
HIGHEST: Wheeler Peak at 13,161 feet (4,011 m)
LOWEST: Red Bluff Reservoir in Eddy County at 2,817 feet (859 m)

• Alamogordo

White Sands National Monument

Carlsbad •

Eddy County

Up to 300,000 bats fly out of Carlsbad Caverns every evening from May through November!

TEXAS

MEXICO

The Rio Grande is New Mexico's major river. It runs through the state from north to south.

TOURING THE CAVES AT CARLSBAD CAVERNS

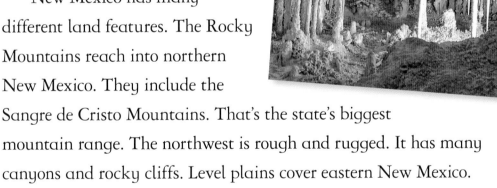

Put on your knee pads. You might find yourself crawling through cave tunnels! You're entering Carlsbad Caverns. But you don't have to crawl. You can stroll along if you'd like.

New Mexico has many different land features. The Rocky Mountains reach into northern New Mexico. They include the Sangre de Cristo Mountains. That's the state's biggest mountain range. The northwest is rough and rugged. It has many canyons and rocky cliffs. Level plains cover eastern New Mexico. Thousands of cattle and sheep graze there.

Deserts cover about 50 percent of the state. Some are rocky, while others are sandy. White Sands National Monument is in the south near Alamogordo. Its sand is—you guessed it—white!

The most visited cave at Carlsbad Caverns is the Big Room.

WHITE SANDS NATIONAL MONUMENT NEAR ALAMOGORDO

White Sands National Monument near Alamogordo is an awesome sight. Its sand almost looks like glistening snow! It stretches as far as the eye can see. Some sand is heaped up in big dunes. In other places, it's in wavy ripples.

Many animals live here. Some animals have developed ways to blend in. One type of mouse and one type of lizard are almost completely white! This coloring protects them in the sand.

People can't visit some parts of the White Sands area. The U.S. government tests missiles there. The first **atomic bomb** was tested there, too.

Visitors enjoy sledding down the sand dunes.

STATE TREE
PIÑON PINE

STATE FLOWER
YUCCA FLOWER

STATE BIRD
**CHAPARRAL
(GREATER ROADRUNNER)**

Slam on the brakes! There goes a roadrunner!

COLORADO

OKLAHOMA

ARIZONA

• Albuquerque

Gila Wilderness

• Silver City

The National Park Service has 18 sites in New Mexico.

Gila Cliff Dwellings National Monument is in Gila Wilderness. The Mogollon people built these homes in the canyon walls more than 700 years ago.

TEXAS

MEXICO

The New Mexico Museum of Natural History and Science in Albuquerque has exhibits about the Southwest.

Gila Wilderness is near Silver City. It was established in 1924. It was the nation's first designated wilderness.

WATCHING WILDLIFE IN GILA WILDERNESS

Hike through the thick forests of Gila Wilderness. *Gila* is pronounced HEE-lah. It's like hiking through an outdoor zoo!

You might see mountain lions, coyotes, and bears. Be still and don't bother them, though. They could be dangerous.

You'll also see deer, antelope, and wild turkeys. You might even see a javelina, or peccary. It's a kind of wild pig.

New Mexico is home to many other animals. Bighorn sheep live in the high mountains. Kangaroo rats live in dry desert regions. They hop really far with their long hind legs.

And don't forget the state bird. It's the greater roadrunner. Beep-beep!

Mule deer can be seen in Gila Wilderness.

CHACO CULTURE NATIONAL HISTORICAL PARK

Think about the building where you live. How many rooms does it have? Imagine a building with more than 600 rooms. That's what **Pueblo** Bonito is like. It's a building in Chaco **Culture** National Historical Park near Nageezi. People called the Ancestral Pueblo built it.

The Ancestral Pueblo lived here more than 1,000 years ago. They built an amazing city. It had buildings, roads, dams, and earthen mounds. The Ancestral Pueblo farmed and hunted. They traded with other peoples for goods they needed.

The Ancestral Pueblo's **descendants** are still alive today. They are called the Pueblo people. They live in New Mexico and Arizona.

Pueblo Bonito had many rooms. You can see them all when you stand up on a cliff!

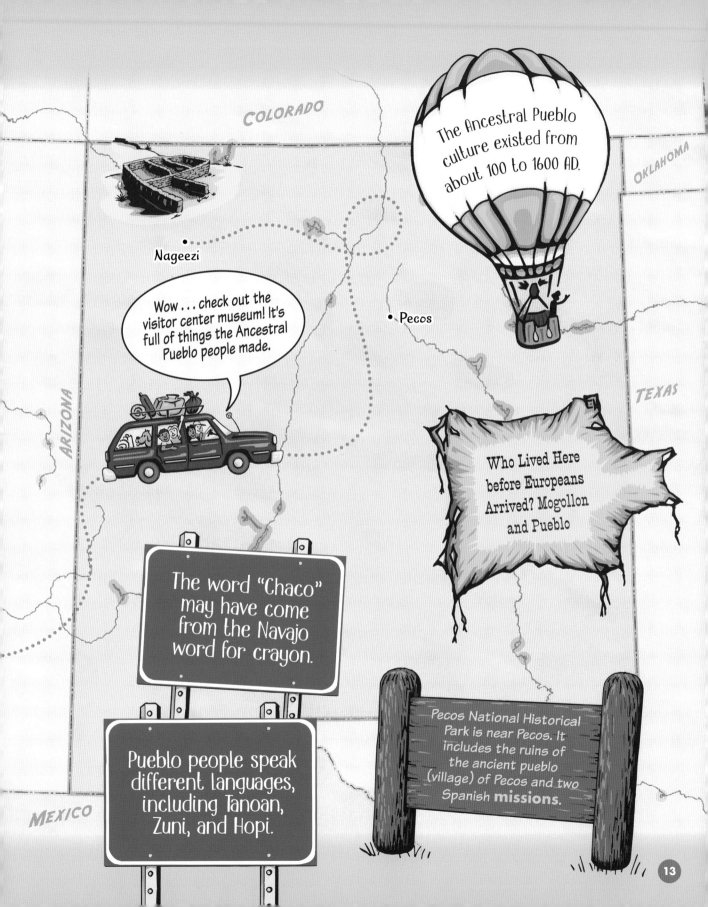

COLORADO

OKLAHOMA

The Ancestral Pueblo culture existed from about 100 to 1600 AD.

Nageezi

Wow . . . check out the visitor center museum! It's full of things the Ancestral Pueblo people made.

• Pecos

TEXAS

ARIZONA

Who Lived Here before Europeans Arrived? Mogollon and Pueblo

The word "Chaco" may have come from the Navajo word for crayon.

Pueblo people speak different languages, including Tanoan, Zuni, and Hopi.

Pecos National Historical Park is near Pecos. It includes the ruins of the ancient pueblo (village) of Pecos and two Spanish **missions**.

MEXICO

COLORADO

OKLAHOMA

New Mexico is home to three Apache tribes, the Navajo Nation, and 19 Pueblos.

Gallup •

ARIZONA

• Rio Rancho

Acoma Pueblo •

• Albuquerque

In 2016, 2,081,015 people lived in New Mexico. It's the 36th-largest state by population.

POPULATION OF LARGEST CITIES
Albuquerque...............559,121
Las Cruces..................101,643
Rio Rancho..................94,171

• Las Cruces

TEXAS

MEXICO

Almost one out of ten New Mexicans is Native American. More than two out of five New Mexicans are Hispanic.

Acoma Pueblo is high on a mesa, or flat-topped hill. People have lived there since at least 1150 AD.

Yum! Let's eat some Navajo fry bread while we watch the rodeo.

GALLUP'S INTER-TRIBAL INDIAN CEREMONIAL

The Inter-Tribal Indian Ceremonial is a dazzling festival. Dozens of Native American groups take part. You'll see them perform **traditional** dances. Their costumes are a swirl of colors! There's a rodeo, complete with bull riding. And you can eat delicious Native American foods.

New Mexico has been largely shaped by Native American, Hispanic, and Anglo cultures. Anglos are white people descended from Europeans.

Some Native Americans live on **reservations**. Others live in pueblos or in New Mexico towns or cities. The major nations are Pueblo, Navajo, and Apache. New Mexico's Hispanics are mainly descended from Spaniards and Mexicans. Their native Spanish language is heard around the state.

Zuni women display traditional clothes and pottery.

SANTA FE'S EL RANCHO DE LAS GOLONDRINAS

A woman makes a long string of chili peppers. It's called a *ristra*. She will hang it up to dry. It's a welcome sign for visitors.

This woman works at El Rancho de las Golondrinas. It's a living history museum. People's clothes and activities show life in the 1700s and 1800s. That's when this rancho, or farm, was built.

Spain ruled New Mexico for more than 200 years. During that time, many Spaniards had ranchos there. Spanish priests opened missions, too. They taught Christianity to Native Americans. The priests also tried to make Native Americans live like the Spaniards did.

New Mexico came under Mexico's rule in 1821. Then Americans and Mexicans fought the Mexican War (1846–1848). The United States won and took over New Mexico.

When you stop by El Rancho de las Golondrinas, visit an old Spanish colonial village.

Ranchos were almost like villages. They had fields, workshops, churches, and schools.

COLORADO

OKLAHOMA

★ Santa Fe

TEXAS

ARIZONA

What are golondrinas? They're swallows! These little birds build their nests at the rancho.

Dear Señor Coronado:
You came to New Mexico in 1540. You thought it might have cities of gold. But that was just a tall tale. You spent seven years searching for those cities.

Sincerely,
Gold C. Kerr

post card

Francisco Vázquez de Coronado
ca. 1510-1554
New Spain

MEXICO

Pueblo Native Americans **revolted** in 1680. They did not want the Spaniards to change their way of life. They drove the Spaniards out of New Mexico. Spain gained control again in 1693.

Mexico was once a Spanish **colony** called New Spain. Mexico gained freedom from Spain in 1821.

DÍA DE LOS MUERTOS IN MESILLA

People are wearing skeleton masks. They're eating candy shaped like skulls. Is this some kind of Halloween festival? In a way, it is. It's Día de los Muertos. That's Spanish for "Day of the Dead."

Halloween, on October 31, began as a Christian holiday. It was the day before All Saints' Day—November 1. The next day is All Souls' Day. That day, November 2, people honor loved ones who have died. It's called Día de los Muertos in Hispanic culture.

Mesilla's celebration is very colorful. Altars to the dead fill the town square. They're decorated with candles, flowers, and photos. It's not a sad festival at all. It's a way to celebrate a loved one's life!

People decorate masks for Día de los Muertos in Mesilla.

Reward—$5,000—Billy the Kid—Dead or Alive!

Billy the Kid was a famous outlaw in the late 1800s. Just visit the Billy the Kid Museum. You'll learn all about his wild life. And you'll see posters offering rewards for his capture.

Billy lived when New Mexico was a U.S. **territory**. He got involved in a war between ranchers. He ended up stealing cattle and killing people.

REWARD

($5,000.00)

Reward for the capture, dead or alive, of one Wm. Wright, better known as

"BILLY THE KID"

Age, 18. Height, 5 feet, 3 inches. Weight, 125 lbs. Light hair, blue eyes and even features. He is the leader of the worst band of desperadoes the Territory has ever had to deal with. The above reward will be paid for his capture or positive proof of his death.

At that time, Native Americans and settlers fought many battles. The Native Americans tried to hold on to their lands. But the settlers defeated them. Apache and Navajo people were forced onto reservations. Apache chief Geronimo kept fighting until 1886, when he was defeated, too.

There was a large reward for anyone who found Billy the Kid.

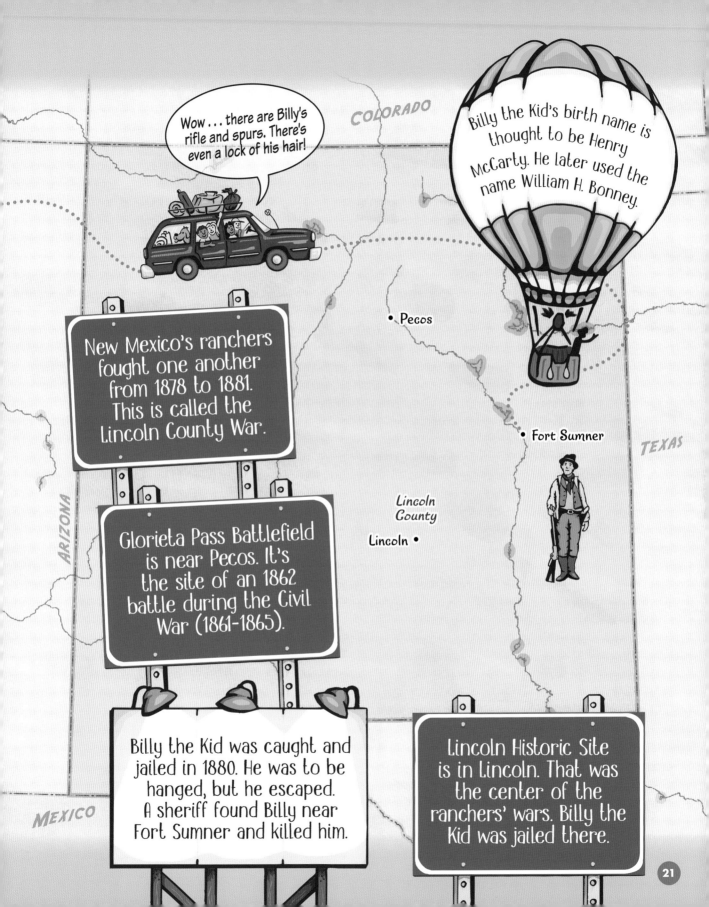

Wow . . . there are Billy's rifle and spurs. There's even a lock of his hair!

Billy the Kid's birth name is thought to be Henry McCarty. He later used the name William H. Bonney.

COLORADO

Pecos

Fort Sumner

TEXAS

Lincoln County

Lincoln

ARIZONA

New Mexico's ranchers fought one another from 1878 to 1881. This is called the Lincoln County War.

Glorieta Pass Battlefield is near Pecos. It's the site of an 1862 battle during the Civil War (1861-1865).

MEXICO

Billy the Kid was caught and jailed in 1880. He was to be hanged, but he escaped. A sheriff found Billy near Fort Sumner and killed him.

Lincoln Historic Site is in Lincoln. That was the center of the ranchers' wars. Billy the Kid was jailed there.

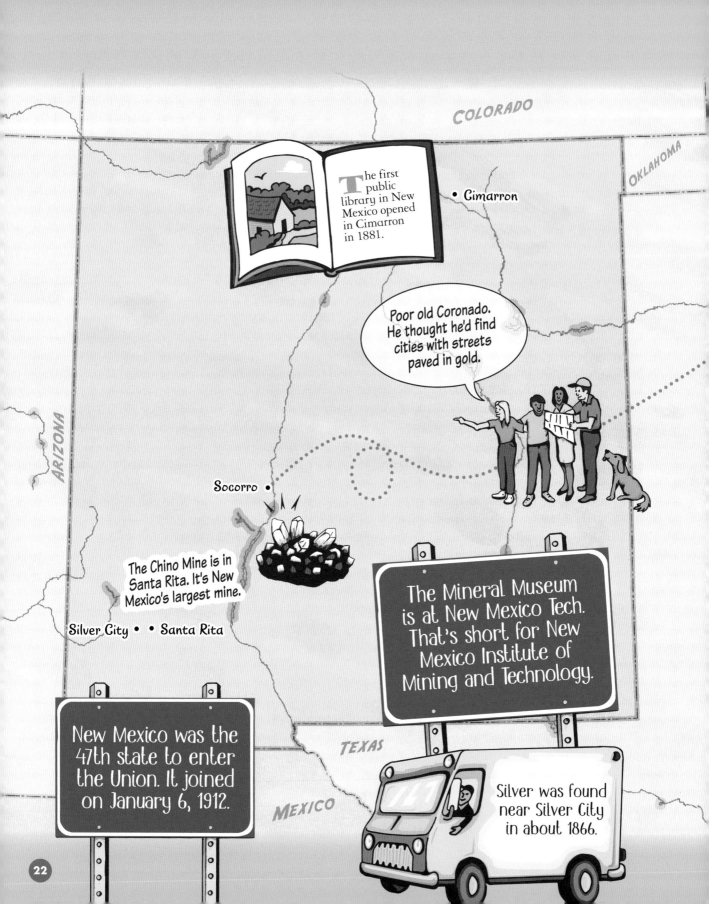

THE MINERAL MUSEUM IN SOCORRO

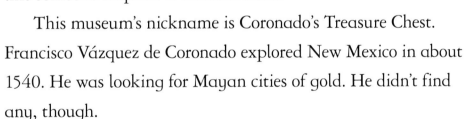

Look around the New Mexico Bureau of Geology and Mineral Resources Mineral Museum. It's a real feast for your eyes. You see gold and silver. Precious gems are sparkling everywhere. It looks like someone emptied a treasure chest!

This museum's nickname is Coronado's Treasure Chest. Francisco Vázquez de Coronado explored New Mexico in about 1540. He was looking for Mayan cities of gold. He didn't find any, though.

Maybe Coronado didn't look hard enough. New Mexicans discovered gold in 1828. More gold was found in the 1860s. Then miners found silver, too.

Mining quickly became a big business in New Mexico. Thousands of people rushed in to get rich. Mining towns sprang up overnight. Many of them shut down just as quickly. They turned into **ghost towns**.

New Mexico produces many beautiful crystals, including fluorite.

Do you like science? Then you'll love Bradbury Science Museum. There are lots of hands-on displays. Every month, scientists give presentations and create activities visitors can try. Visitors can also try to solve puzzles that require them to use different thinking styles.

Los Alamos National Laboratory operates this museum. Scientists worked at Los Alamos in the 1940s. They developed the first atomic bomb.

New Mexico's science activities kept growing. Sandia National Laboratories opened in Albuquerque. Scientists there work with **nuclear energy**.

Scientists at Los Alamos are still working, too. They're finding new ways to use nuclear energy.

See a replica of one of the World War II atomic bombs at Bradbury Science Museum.

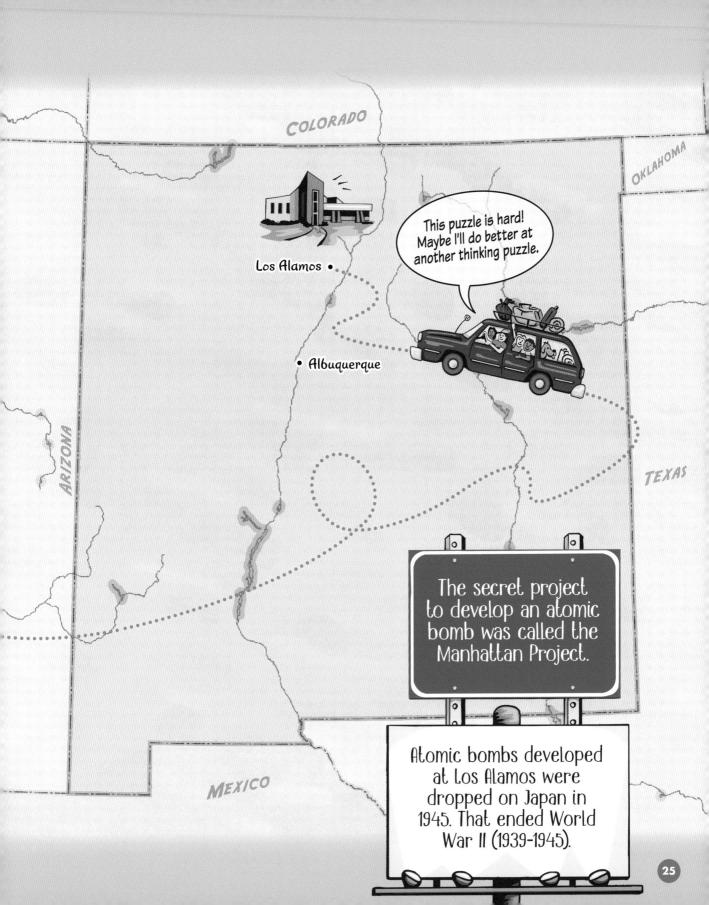

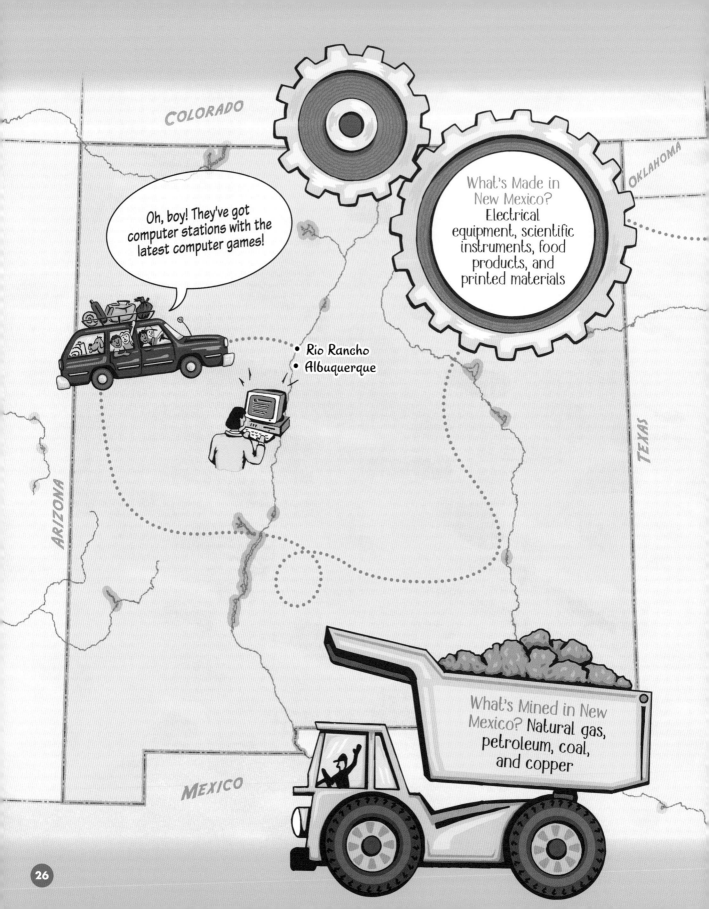

INTEL COMPUTERS AT RIO RANCHO

Intel is a big computer company near Albuquerque in Rio Rancho. It makes computer chips. Those are tiny parts that make computers work.

Stop by the Intel Visitors Center. It's like a computer museum. The first thing you see is a bunny suit. That's what it's called, anyhow. Workers wear these suits in the factory. This keeps the computer chips super clean!

Computer equipment is one of New Mexico's major factory products. Some factories make food. Clothes and many other goods are also made there.

Mining is a big business, too. New Mexico once mined lots of gold and silver. Today, it mines oil and natural gas. Miners are also digging out coal and copper.

An Intel worker helps high school students learn about computers.

SWIMMING IN SANTA ROSA'S BLUE HOLE

Dive into the clear blue water. You see goldfish swimming around you! You're in a deep pool called the Blue Hole. It's a favorite spot for divers.

New Mexico has plenty of places to have fun. Swimmers and boaters love Santa Rosa's lakes. The Blue Hole is just one of them.

Some people enjoy New Mexico's deserts. They see cactus and lots of desert animals. Others like to climb rocks and mountains. In the winter, snow falls in the mountains. Then people ski down the snowy slopes.

Many towns have rodeos. Real cowboys come to show off their skills. And there are festivals all year long. They celebrate New Mexico's many cultures.

The Blue Hole is 82 feet (25 m) deep.

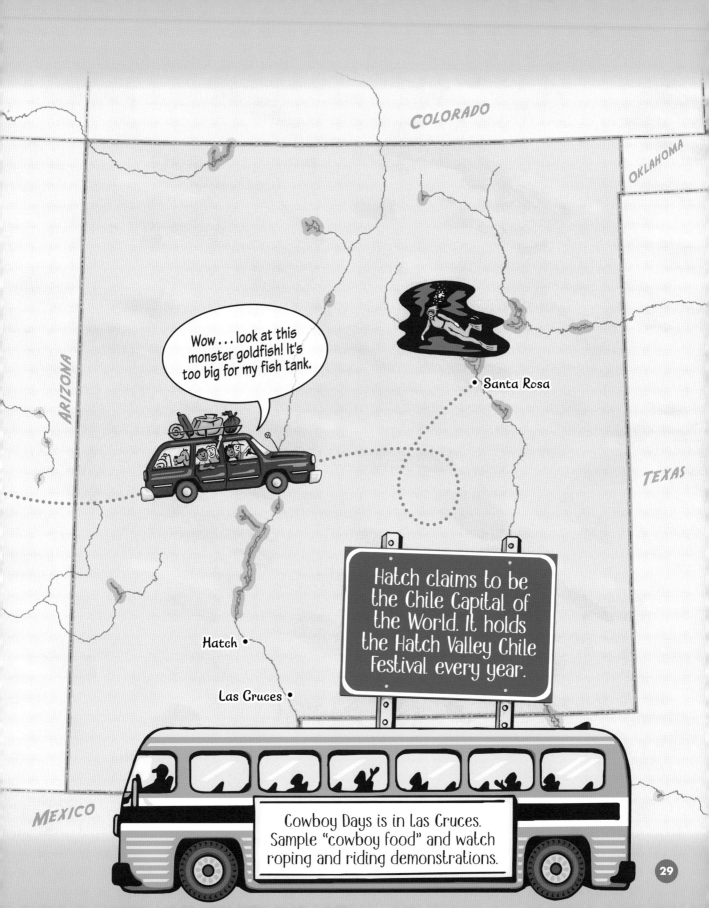

New Mexico's state motto is "Crescit eundo." This is Latin for "It grows as it goes."

Santa Fe

Santa Fe's New Mexico History Museum includes the Palace of the Governors, the building the Spanish made to house their government when they controlled the American Southwest.

Hey, look! You can go in through doorways on four sides. That's like the four directions on the Zia.

ARIZONA

OKLAHOMA

TEXAS

MEXICO

Welcome to Santa Fe, the capital of New Mexico!

Santa Fe became the capital of New Mexico in about 1610. It's the oldest capital city in the United States.

The capitol is shaped like a kiva. That's a Pueblo Native American room for religious ceremonies. A kiva is partly underground, and so is the capitol.

THE STATE CAPITOL IN SANTA FE

New Mexico's state capitol is called the Roundhouse. Just visit it, and you'll see why. It's round! It's built in the shape of the Zia.

The Zia is a very old Pueblo Native American symbol. It stands for the Sun. Rays shine from the top, bottom, and sides. They stand for the four directions and the four seasons.

Inside the capitol are the state government offices. New Mexico has three branches of government. One branch makes the state's laws. The governor leads another branch. It carries out the laws. Judges make up the third branch. They decide whether someone has broken the law.

One of the Roundhouse's four stories is underground.

THE FARM AND RANCH HERITAGE MUSEUM IN LAS CRUCES

Watch a farmer milk a cow and a blacksmith make iron tools. Then learn about the many breeds of beef cattle that live at the museum.

You're visiting the New Mexico Farm and Ranch Heritage Museum in Las Cruces. It shows how New Mexicans farmed for 4,000 years.

Farming has always been important to New Mexico. Early peoples grew corn, beans, and squash. These are known as the three sisters. Today, cattle ranching is the top farm activity. Thousands of cattle graze across the eastern plains. Many ranchers raise sheep, too.

Hay, chili peppers, and onions are leading crops. Crops grow best in the river valleys. Water is brought to the fields through **irrigation**.

You might see a newborn calf at the Farm and Ranch Heritage Museum.

THE INTERNATIONAL UFO MUSEUM IN ROSWELL

Do you believe in UFOs? That stands for unidentified flying objects. If you do, you've got to visit Roswell. Head straight for the International UFO Museum and Research Center!

Many people believe a UFO crashed in Roswell. They believe it was a spaceship. They think aliens were aboard. What became of these creatures from another planet? That's what everyone is wondering.

Believe the story or not. It's for you to decide! In any case, you'll enjoy the museum. You'll learn about UFO sightings around the world. You'll see exhibits about the Roswell crash. And you'll learn about lots of other weird happenings. How can you resist?

The UFO Museum is the place to go if you want information on UFOs!

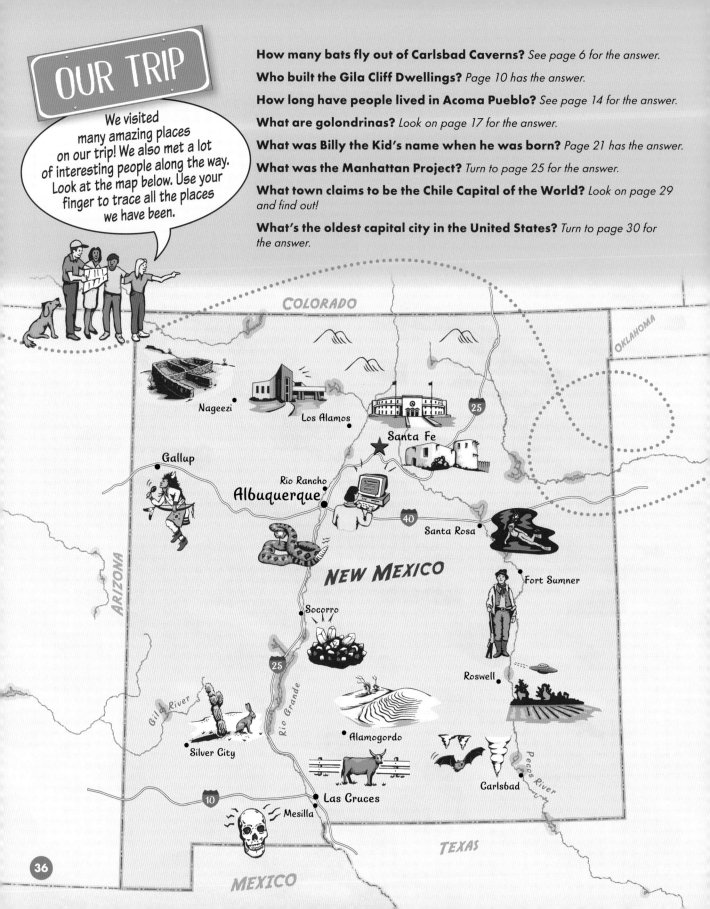

OUR TRIP

We visited many amazing places on our trip! We also met a lot of interesting people along the way. Look at the map below. Use your finger to trace all the places we have been.

How many bats fly out of Carlsbad Caverns? *See page 6 for the answer.*

Who built the Gila Cliff Dwellings? *Page 10 has the answer.*

How long have people lived in Acoma Pueblo? *See page 14 for the answer.*

What are golondrinas? *Look on page 17 for the answer.*

What was Billy the Kid's name when he was born? *Page 21 has the answer.*

What was the Manhattan Project? *Turn to page 25 for the answer.*

What town claims to be the Chile Capital of the World? *Look on page 29 and find out!*

What's the oldest capital city in the United States? *Turn to page 30 for the answer.*

COLORADO

OKLAHOMA

ARIZONA

Nageezi

Los Alamos

Santa Fe

25

Gallup

Rio Rancho

Albuquerque

40

Santa Rosa

Fort Sumner

NEW MEXICO

Socorro

Roswell

25

Gila River

Rio Grande

Silver City

Alamogordo

Las Cruces

Mesilla

10

Carlsbad

Pecos River

TEXAS

MEXICO

State flag

State seal

That was a great trip! We have traveled all over New Mexico! There are a few places we didn't have time for, though. Next time, we plan to visit the American International Rattlesnake Museum in Albuquerque. The museum is home to snakes from North, Central, and South America. It contains the world's largest live collection of different types of rattlesnakes.

STATE SYMBOLS

State animal: Black bear

State bird: Chaparral (greater roadrunner)

State cookie: Bizcochito

State fish: Native New Mexico cutthroat trout

State flower: Yucca flower

State fossil: Coelophysis

State gem: Turquoise

State grass: Blue grama

State insect: Tarantula hawk wasp

State tree: Piñon pine

State vegetables: Chile and frijole

STATE SONG

"O, FAIR NEW MEXICO"

Words and music by Elizabeth Garrett, daughter of Pat Garrett, the legendary sheriff who killed Billy the Kid

Under a sky of azure, where balmy breezes blow;
Kissed by the golden sunshine, is Nuevo Mejico.
Home of the Montezuma, with fiery heart aglow,
State of the deeds historic, is Nuevo Mejico.

Chorus:
O, fair New Mexico, we love, we love you so,
Our hearts with pride o'erflow,
No matter where we go.
O, fair New Mexico, we love, we love you so,
The grandest state to know—New Mexico.

Rugged and high sierras, with deep canyons below;
Dotted with fertile valleys, is Nuevo Mejico.
Fields full of sweet alfalfa, richest perfumes bestow,
State of apple blossoms, is Nuevo Mejico.

Days that are full of heart-dreams, nights when the
Moon hangs low;
Beaming its benediction o'er Nuevo Mejico.
Land with its bright mañana, coming through weal and
woe; State of our esperanza, is Nuevo Mejico.

FAMOUS PEOPLE

Adams, Ansel (1902–1984), photographer

Anaya, Rudolfo (1937–), children's author

Blume, Judy (1938–), children's author

Bunche, Ralph (1904–1971), Nobel Peace Prize recipient and diplomat

Carson, Christopher "Kit" (1809–1868), hunter and guide

Chavez, Dennis (1888–1962), politician and humanitarian

Ferguson, Jesse Tyler (1975–), actor

Geronimo (1829–1909), Apache leader

Goddard, Robert H. (1882–1945), rocket scientist

Gutierrez, Sid (1951–), astronaut

Hanna, William (1910–2001), cartoonist

Harris, Neil Patrick (1973–), actor

Hilton, Conrad N. (1887–1979), hotel executive

James, Rebecca Salsbury (1891–1968), artist

Lamy, Jean-Baptiste (1814–1888), Catholic archbishop and humanitarian

Lopez, Nancy (1957–), professional golfer

Martinez, Maria (ca. 188?–1980), potter

McCarty, Henry "Billy the Kid" (1859–1881), famous outlaw

Moore, Demi (1962–), actress

O'Keeffe, Georgia (1887–1986), artist

Popé (ca. 1630–ca. 1692), Pueblo hero

Unser, Bobby (1934–), **Al Sr.** (1939–), **Al Jr.** (1962–), auto racers

Victorio (ca. 1825–1880), Apache chief

WORDS TO KNOW

atomic bomb (uh-TOM-ik BOM) a powerful bomb made by splitting tiny particles called atoms

colony (KOL-uh-nee) a land with ties to another country

culture (KUHL-chur) a people's customs, beliefs, and ways of life

descendants (di-SEND-uhnts) children, grandchildren, great-grandchildren, and so on

ghost towns (GOHST TOUNS) towns where everyone has moved out

irrigation (ihr-ruh-GAY-shuhn) a way of bringing water to fields through pipes or ditches

missions (MISH-uhnz) centers where religious people try to spread their faith

nuclear energy (NOO-clee-ur EN-ur-jee) the energy released when atoms are split

pueblo (PWEB-loh) a village or a Native American building with many homes inside

reservations (rez-ur-VAY-shuhnz) lands where the U.S. government forced Native American groups to move

revolted (ree-VOHLT-ed) rebelled against a government or ruler

territory (TER-i-tor-ee) land outside of a country that is controlled by the country

traditional (truh-DISH-uh-nul) following long-held customs

TO LEARN MORE

IN THE LIBRARY

Bjorklund, Ruth. *New Mexico*. 2nd ed. New York, NY: Marshall Cavendish, 2013.

Buellis, Linda. *Pueblo*. New York, NY: PowerKids Press, 2016.

Coleman, Miriam. *New Mexico: The Land of Enchantment*. New York, NY: PowerKids Press, 2011.

Lyon, Robin. *The Spanish Missions of New Mexico*. New York, NY: Children's Press, 2010.

ON THE WEB
Visit our Web site for links about New Mexico:
childsworld.com/links

Note to Parents, Teachers, and Librarians: We routinely verify our Web links to make sure they are safe and active sites. So encourage your readers to check them out!

PLACES TO VISIT OR CONTACT
Historical Society of New Mexico
hsnm.org
PO Box 1912
Santa Fe, NM 87504
For more information about the history of New Mexico

New Mexico Tourism Department
newmexico.org
491 Old Santa Fe Trail
Santa Fe, NM 87501
505/827-7400
For more information about traveling in New Mexico

New Mexico covers 121,590 square miles (314,917 sq km). It's the 5th-largest state in size.

INDEX

Bye, Land of Enchantment. We had a great time. We'll come back soon!